Powerful
People
Are
Powerful
Networkers

Powerful People
Are
Powerful Networkers

Your Daily Guide
To Becoming A Powerful Person

Peter Biadasz and Richard Possett

iUniverse, Inc.
New York Lincoln Shanghai

Powerful People Are Powerful Networkers
Your Daily Guide To Becoming A Powerful Person

iUniverse books may be ordered through booksellers or by contacting:

iUniverse
2021 Pine Lake Road, Suite 100
Lincoln, NE 68512
www.iuniverse.com
1-800-Authors (1-800-288-4677)

ISBN-13: 978-0-595-37723-7 (pbk)
ISBN-13: 978-0-595-82102-0 (ebk)
ISBN-10: 0-595-37723-8 (pbk)
ISBN-10: 0-595-82102-2 (ebk)

Printed in the United States of America

The wisdom of the wise, and the experience of the ages, may be preserved by quotation.

Benjamin Disraeli

Dedications

This book is dedicated to Stewart L. Brenner, who is living proof that a high school teacher can instill and teach discipline, work ethic and the drive to be "number one" to a student eager to learn.

—Peter Biadasz

This book is dedicated to all the hard working networkers, who work smartly at networking both themselves and their businesses for fun and profit.

—Richard Possett

Acknowledgements

Thank you to my family, my friends and business associates; you add so much to my personal and professional life. Even though I may not always show it, know that my appreciation runs very deep.

—Peter Biadasz

I say many, many thanks to my wife of forty-one years, Marilyn, and our three children (Nicole, Richard and Michael); son-in-law Daryl; and, my two grandchildren (Braden and Rebekah) for putting up with my occasional foible and folly.

—Richard Possett

Why Read This Book?

POWERFUL PEOPLE ARE POWERFUL NETWORKERS: *Your Daily Guide To Becoming A Powerful Person* is the book for you if you want to add power to all of your relationships. For, in the real world, both personally and professionally, it is not who you know, but who knows you. And, these interpersonal relationships help you to be more efficient and effective in your daily life. The more vast your connections, the more you get things done. Thus, your success is about being productive. It's about immediate results. It's about being connected. It's about being powerful.

Do you want to be a more powerful person; powerful at home, work and play? Of course, your answer is a powerful YES! But, real power is not physical strength. Real power is the knack of getting along; having people like you; and, working with others for bilateral benefit. It's the capacity to make friends, create relationships and influence people. Real power is having an extensive "circle of influence" enabling you to get things done right—right now. It's the ability to motive others for "win-win" situations and mutual advantage.

Right now you are reading a one of a kind book. There is nothing else like it on the bookshelf. This book is unique because of its multidimensional nature. It is a <u>practical</u>, <u>inspirational</u> and <u>educational</u> workbook on networking. Although the book is comprehensively powerful, it is still simple and easy. It's simple to read. And, the work is easy to complete. It's the way to utilize your full potential. The book is a once a day excursion into becoming a proactive networker and thus, a more powerful person.

Read this book; engage the material; and, actualize the subject matter. By the time you are done, you will be a more powerful person with new found strengths in your personal and professional relationships. As you progress through this book, you will discover both your good networking customs and bad networking habits. You will grow more powerful each day by building on your strengths and eliminating your weaknesses.

Through the daily lessons, you learn an inspirational quote. By completing the daily lessons, you become a more knowledgeable and effective networker. When you research the authors, you become a well rounded individual. By being a more conversant, learned and interesting person, you become more powerful to all those around you and your "circle of influence."

A bonus in the book is that you can reflect upon your work after six months. This process gives you an honest chance to critique your investment and make the appropriate adjustments. It enhances and reinforces your networking efforts for better results in your private and professional life. By learning the daily lessons and applying one skill each day into your business and personal world, you will become a master networker reaping wonderful individual and financial rewards. Work on it and make it work! <u>Become a powerful person through powerful networking.</u>

Contents

Preface

In some form or fashion, we have networked our entire lives. It has been the foundation of our livelihood. For us, networking is a tried and true way of "making friends and influencing people" to purchase our goods and services. Whether you are a product producer or service provider, networking can help immeasurably to increase your sales. If it doesn't, then truly you are not networking the right way.

The principles in this book have been born of two long and productive business careers. We walk the walk. We practice what we preach. We are confident that the quotations in this book will inspire you to do the same. It should take you beyond mediocrity in both business and at home. As they are completed, the daily lessons will make you a more dynamic networker. Please read and fill in the blanks for your life and enjoy. We pray that you have a great day and a better tomorrow as you network your way to awesome success.

Peter Biadasz and Richard Possett

(Before proceeding, turn to pages 187 and 188 to read more about the authors and gain a better frame of reference and perspective regarding this book.)

Introduction

What Is Networking?

Networking is nothing more than people interacting with each other. While we are all networkers, everyone is at a different level of networking proficiency. The best networkers are very effective in helping meet the needs of others by utilizing people in their network to create win-win situations. Your network is everyone that you know and who knows you. At its best, your network is your total personal resource and professional marketing department. Likewise, as a proficient networker you are a total resource for everyone that you come in contact with. How thorough a resource you are depends on the strength and depth of your network. The more powerful you are as a person, the more powerful your network. The more powerful your network, the more powerful you are as a person.

What (Or Who) Is A Powerful Person?

A powerful person is anyone who has influence over another person. Notice that we said influence, not control. Many people misunderstand power as a control issue. Whether you know it or not, you influence many people every day. It may be as obvious as your interaction with a co-worker or a family member; or, as subtle as your mannerisms when standing in a long checkout line at the store. In every circumstance where you can be observed by another person, you are exerting influence by word and/or by example. This book will address the characteristics that you show to the people in your life. These are the same characteristics that these same people look at when determining how powerful a person you are to them. The powerful people quoted in this book were powerful because of their influence on others, even you. Yet you may have never met any one of these individuals, just as you may not have met many of the people that you have affected, either positively or negatively.

In the margin of this page take a minute now and list the most powerful influences in your life. This is where your powerful lifestyle example begins.

How To Use This Book

Everyday you are given the opportunity to be more proficient in a networking skill that leads you to become a more powerful person. Read the daily quote and then thoughtfully complete the task presented.

Six Months Review

The six months review gives you the opportunity to add depth to what you have learned and to the task that you had started—and hopefully completed six months earlier. This is critical to ensure that networking habits, not just actions, are created and reinforced. At the end of one year, you will find that you have addressed all of the major areas that make you a powerful networker.

To reinforce certain key points, you may see a topic covered more than once. Note that this is a key topic requiring your thorough and honest attention.

Sample Illustration

January 1
July 1

> "Go forth into the busy world and love it.
> Interest yourself in life, mingle kindly with
> its joys and sorrows, try what you can do
> for others rather than what you can make
> them do for you, and you will know what it
> is to have friends."

Ralph Waldo Emerson

Record the names of two people and then list specific networking activities
(lunch, lead, referral, visit, etc.) that you are going to do with them this week.

Name: _Joyce Fordson_

Activity: _Telephone Joyce and schedule a lunch to discuss the status of the_
Gorden and Gloria Golden home purchase transaction referral.

Name: _Ed Gomezsky_

Activity: _Contact Ed and set an appointment to visit his office, tour the_
facilities and meet his staff and colleagues.

Six Months Review:
We followed the Golden deal and it closed three months ago. It had a couple of problems that initially disappointed the Golden's, but we placated them with sweetened terms and conditions. We visited Ed's place of business that same week and developed a good relationship with a colleague.

About The Quote Sources

If you want to receive more rewards from these daily exercises, perform research on the people quoted in these pages. You are encouraged to learn about their life and times. Learning how these individuals became powerful people in their own right will be a great reward. If a person is quoted more than once, research the circumstances in which each quote occurred. When the quote source is a proverb; a study into the traditions associated with each proverb may be of benefit. The results of your research can be placed in the lines provided and labeled as "Quotation Source Information."

Tell me...I'll forget.

Show me...I'll remember.

Involve me...I'll comprehend.

HAPPY NETWORKING!

Important Note

Please understand that in instances in which a quote refers to "him", that the word "her" can be substituted.

January 1
July 2

"A generous person will prosper."

Solomon

List three people that you will be generous to today and detail how you will be generous:

Name: _____
Generosity: _____
_____

Name: _____
Generosity: _____
_____

Name: _____
Generosity: _____
_____

Six Months Review:

_____
_____
_____

Quotation Source Information:

_____
_____
_____

January 2
July 3

"The best way to get a lead
is to give a lead."

Peter Biadasz

List two people that you will give at least one lead to today:

Name: _____

Lead: _____

_____

Name: _____

Lead: _____

_____

Six Months Review:

_____

_____

_____

Quotation Source Information:

_____

_____

_____

January 3
July 4

> "Don't say you don't have enough time. You
> have exactly the same number of hours per
> day that were given to Helen Keller, Pasteur,
> Michelangelo, Mother Theresa, Leonardo
> DaVinci, Thomas Jefferson and Albert
> Einstein."

H. Jackson Brown

Name three things you can do today to improve your time management
skills:

1. _____
   _____

2. _____
   _____

3. _____
   _____

Six Months Review:
_____
_____
_____

Quotation Source Information:
_____
_____
_____

January 4
July 5

"Leave nothing for tomorrow
which can be done today."

Abraham Lincoln

List two things that you <u>must</u> do today:

1. _____
   _____

2. _____
   _____

Six Months Review:

_____
_____
_____

Quotation Source Information:

_____
_____
_____

January 5
July 6

"Associate yourself with men of good quality if you esteem your own reputation."

George Washington

List three people you know that have a solid reputation and form a win/win relationship with each of them:

1. _____
   _____

2. _____
   _____

3. _____
   _____

Six Months Review:

_____
_____
_____

Quotation Source Information:

_____
_____
_____

January 6
July 7

"In networking, as in living life,
always abide by GET = GIVE.
It's the golden rule of networking."

Richard Possett

Think about and reflect upon this tenet and then note how you do or
don't make it part of your networking.

Notes:
_____
_____
_____

Six Months Review:
_____
_____
_____

Quotation Source Information:
_____
_____
_____

January 7
July 8

"Give without remembering and take without forgetting."

Unknown

List three people that you will thank today for what they have done for you:

1. _____
   _____

2. _____
   _____

3. _____
   _____

Six Months Review:

_____
_____
_____

January 8
July 9

"Education is not the filling of a pail,
but the lighting of a fire."

William Butler Yeats

List five things that you are passionate about:

1. _____
   _____

2. _____
   _____

3. _____
   _____

4. _____
   _____

5. _____
   _____

Next to each passion, list someone that you can share that passion with.

Six Months Review:

_____
_____
_____

Quotation Source Information:

_____
_____
_____

January 9
July 10

"Don't be afraid to go out on a limb.
That's where the fruit is."

H. Jackson Brown

List three successes that you feel are just beyond your grasp. What is keeping you from achieving those successes?

1. _____
   _____

2. _____
   _____

3. _____
   _____

Six Months Review:

_____
_____
_____

Quotation Source Information:

_____
_____
_____

January 10
July 11

"Things do not happen,
they are made to happen."

John F. Kennedy

List two things that you are going to make happen today:

1. _____
   _____

2. _____
   _____

Six Months Review:
_____
_____
_____

Quotation Source Information:
_____
_____
_____

January 11
July 12

When you have given nothing,
ask for nothing.

Albanian Proverb

Are you a giver or a taker? (circle one)   Giver   Taker

From who in your network have you earned the right to ask for leads?

_____

_____

_____

Six Months Review:

_____

_____

_____

Quotation Source Information:

_____

_____

_____

January 12
July 13

> "My formula for success is rise early,
> work late and strike oil."

J. Paul Getty

List three things that you can do to improve your work habits:

1. _____
   _____

2. _____
   _____

3. _____
   _____

What is your goal for today?
_____
_____

Six Months Review:
_____
_____
_____

Quotation Source Information:
_____
_____
_____

January 13
July 14

> "If what you are working for really matters,
> you'll give it all you've got."

Nido Qubein

List three things in your work that really matter:

1. _____
   _____

2. _____
   _____

3. _____
   _____

Six Months Review:

_____
_____
_____

Quotation Source Information:

_____
_____
_____

January 14
July 15

> "People prefer to follow those who help
> them, not those who intimidate them."

C. Gene Wilkes

List three ways in which you help people:

1. _____
   _____

2. _____
   _____

3. _____
   _____

Six Months Review:

_____
_____
_____

Quotation Source Information:

_____
_____
_____

January 15
July 16

> "Motivation is what gets you started,
> habit is what keeps you going."

Unknown

List three things that motivate you:

1. _____

2. _____

3. _____

List three of your best habits:

1. _____

2. _____

3. _____

List three of your worst habits and how you can eliminate them:

1. _____

2. _____

3. _____

Six Months Review:

_____

_____

_____

He who is ashamed of asking
is ashamed of learning.

Danish Proverb

List three questions that you wish you had the answers to:

1. _____
   _____

2. _____
   _____

3. _____
   _____

Now list and seek out those people that can answer these questions.

Six Months Review:

_____
_____
_____

Quotation Source Information:

_____
_____
_____

January 17
July 18

> "A wise man will make more
> opportunities than he finds."

Francis Bacon

List one way that you can make an opportunity today to achieve one of
your goals:

_____
_____
_____

Six Months Review:

_____
_____
_____

Quotation Source Information:

_____
_____
_____

January 18
July 19

Talk doesn't cook rice.

Chinese Proverb

Are you a talker or a doer? (circle one)   Talker   Doer

List three things that you have been talking about doing yet have not done:

1. _____
   _____

2. _____
   _____

3. _____
   _____

Today write an action plan to accomplish each thing listed.

Six Months Review:
_____
_____
_____

Quotation Source Information:
_____
_____
_____

January 19
July 20

"A man too busy to take care of his health
is like a mechanic too busy to take
care of his tools."

Spanish Proverb

List three things you can do today to improve your health:

1. _____

_____

2. _____

_____

3. _____

_____

Six Months Review:

_____

_____

_____

Quotation Source Information:

_____

_____

_____

January 20
July 21

"You know more people than you think you know."

Peter Biadasz

During the next 90 days, make a list of everyone you have known from high school to the present. On the lines below, list everyone you have had contact with in the last 24 hours.

_____
_____
_____
_____

Six Months Review:

_____
_____
_____

Quotation Source Information:

_____
_____
_____

January 21
July 22

> "Speak-up about you and what you do in
> life. In networking, never be afraid to *toot*
> your horn and *tout* your business."

Richard Possett

Write a new thirty-second commercial for your business in the space
provided below and then ask a master networker to review it for effectiveness:

_____

_____

_____

Six Months Review:

_____

_____

_____

Quotation Source Information:

_____

_____

_____

January 22
July 23

"Many a live wire would be a dead one
except for connections."

Unknown

List five of your strongest business connections, let them know you appreciate them:

1. _____

_____

2. _____

_____

3. _____

_____

4. _____

_____

5. _____

_____

Six Months Review:

_____

_____

_____

January 23
July 24

> "Ninety-nine percent of failures
> come from people who have
> a habit of making excuses."

George Washington Carver

What is your number one excuse?

_____

_____

_____

Resolve to never utilize that excuse again.

Six Months Review:

_____

_____

_____

Quotation Source Information:

_____

_____

_____

January 24
July 25

"Whenever I meet someone,
I try to imagine him wearing a sign
that says make me feel important."

Mary Kay Ash

Who did you make feel important yesterday? Who are you going to make feel important today?

Yesterday:
_____

Today:
_____

Six Months Review:
_____
_____
_____

Quotation Source Information:
_____
_____
_____

January 25
July 26

"If you can't feed a hundred people, then feed just one."

Mother Teresa

List one person that you will contact today to give a lead to that will add to their personal or professional life:

_____

_____

_____

_____

Six Months Review:

_____

_____

_____

Quotation Source Information:

_____

_____

_____

January 26
July 27

> "I don't have an attitude problem,
> you have a perception problem."

Unknown

List three things that you can do to improve your attitude:

1. _____
   _____

2. _____
   _____

3. _____
   _____

Six Months Review:

_____
_____
_____

January 27
July 28

"The world is full of willing people, some
willing to work, the rest willing to let them."

Unknown

List three of the hardest workers that you know:

1. _____

   _____

2. _____

   _____

3. _____

   _____

Are you one of the people that you listed? (circle one)   Yes   No

Why or why not?

_____

_____

Six Months Review:

_____

_____

_____

January 28
July 29

"If advertisers spent the same amount of money on improving their products as they do on advertising, then they would not have to advertise them."

Will Rogers

How can you improve your word of mouth advertising?

_____
_____
_____
_____
_____

Six Months Review:

_____
_____
_____

Quotation Source Information:

_____
_____
_____

January 29
July 30

"The only difference between a rut and a grave is their dimensions."

Unknown

List two ruts that you are in and one thing you can do today to get out of these ruts:

1. _____
   _____

2. _____
   _____

Six Months Review:

_____
_____
_____

January 30
July 31

> "Those who want milk should not sit on a
> stool in the middle of a field waiting for a
> cow to walk up to them."

Unknown

List three people in your network to whom you will give business and receive leads.

1. _____
   _____

2. _____
   _____

3. _____
   _____

Six Months Review:

_____
_____
_____

January 31
August 1

> "He whose ranks are united in purpose
> will be victorious."

Sun Tzu

List five people that you can call on anytime to receive leads.

1. _____
   _____

2. _____
   _____

3. _____
   _____

4. _____
   _____

5. _____
   _____

Six Months Review:

_____
_____
_____

Quotation Source Information:

_____
_____
_____

February 1
August 2

> "Networking is not about you,
> it's not about me—it's about us."

Peter Biadasz

List your five strongest networking contacts:

1. _____
   _____

2. _____
   _____

3. _____
   _____

4. _____
   _____

5. _____
   _____

Six Months Review:

_____
_____
_____

Quotation Source Information:

_____
_____
_____

February 2
August 3

> "A pessimist sees the difficulty in every opportunity; an optimist sees the opportunity in every difficulty."

Winston Churchill

List three challenges that you are facing and the opportunities that will arise as a result of facing and conquering these challenges:

1. _____
   _____

2. _____
   _____

3. _____
   _____

Six Months Review:

_____
_____
_____

Quotation Source Information:

_____
_____
_____

February 3
August 4

> "As you walk down the fairway of life you must smell the roses, for you only get to play one round."

> **Ben Hogan**

List three things that you really appreciate about your life:

1. _____
   _____

2. _____
   _____

3. _____
   _____

Six Months Review:

_____
_____
_____

Quotation Source Information:

_____
_____
_____

February 4
August 5

> "The talent for discovering the unique and marketable characteristics of a product and service is a designer's most valuable asset."

Primo Angeli

List three *unique* characteristics of your product or service and ways that you market these characteristics:

1. _____
   _____

2. _____
   _____

3. _____
   _____

Six Months Review:

_____
_____
_____

Quotation Source Information:

_____
_____
_____

February 5
August 6

"The best preparation for tomorrow is to
do today's work superbly well."

William Olsen

List three things that you are going to do superbly today:

1. _____
   _____

2. _____
   _____

3. _____
   _____

Six Months Review:
_____
_____
_____

Quotation Source Information:
_____
_____
_____

February 6
August 7

"He who angers you conquers you."

Elizabeth Kenny

List one person that angers you:

_____
_____
_____
_____

Today, resolve the circumstances at the root of the anger.

Six Months Review:

_____
_____
_____

Quotation Source Information:

_____
_____
_____

February 7
August 8

"Always do more than is required of you."

George S. Patton

List three things you can do today that are above and beyond what you are expected to do:

1. _____
   _____

2. _____
   _____

3. _____
   _____

Six Months Review:

_____
_____
_____

Quotation Source Information:

_____
_____
_____

February 8
August 9

"The secret of living is giving."

Unknown

List three ways that you can give to another today. List their names:

1. _____
   _____

2. _____
   _____

3. _____
   _____

Six Months Review:

_____
_____
_____

February 9
August 10

> "My mother said to me, 'If you become a soldier, you'll be a general; if you become a monk, you'll end up as the Pope.' Instead, I became a painter and wound up as Picasso."

Pablo Picasso

At what do you want to be the best?

_____
_____
_____
_____

Six Months Review:

_____
_____
_____

Quotation Source Information:

_____
_____
_____

February 10
August 11

"Never grow a wishbone where your backbone ought to be."

Clementine Paddleford

List one thing that you have been wishing for and write down how you will achieve that wish:

_____
_____
_____
_____

Six Months Review:

_____
_____
_____

Quotation Source Information:

_____
_____
_____

February 11
August 12

> "A positive attitude may not solve all your
> problems, but it will annoy enough people
> to make it worth the effort."

Herm Albright

List three of the most positive people that you know. Ask them their secrets for staying positive and write the secrets on the lines below:

1. _____
   _____

2. _____
   _____

3. _____
   _____

Six Months Review:

_____
_____
_____

Quotation Source Information:

_____
_____
_____

February 12
August 13

"There are two ways of spreading light—to
be the candle or the mirror that reflects it."

Edith Wharton

List ways in which you are a candle (initiator) and a mirror (follower):

Initiator:

_____

_____

Follower:

_____

_____

Six Months Review:

_____

_____

_____

Quotation Source Information:

_____

_____

_____

February 13
August 14

There is no pillow so soft as a
clear conscience.

French Proverb

List all the things in your life that you feel guilty about:

_____
_____
_____
_____

Resolve each item immediately.

Six Months Review:

_____
_____
_____

Quotation Source Information:

_____
_____
_____

February 14
August 15

"To make headway, improve your head."

B.C. Forbes

List five ways that you will improve your head today:

1. _____

   _____

2. _____

   _____

3. _____

   _____

4. _____

   _____

5. _____

   _____

Six Months Review:

_____

_____

_____

Quotation Source Information:

_____

_____

_____

February 15
August 16

> "A professional is a person who can do his
> best at a time when he doesn't particularly
> feel like it."

Alistair Cooke

How do you appear to always be at your best, even when not feeling your best?

_____

_____

_____

Six Months Review:

_____

_____

_____

Quotation Source Information:

_____

_____

_____

February 16
August 17

"Opportunity is missed by most people
because it comes dressed in overalls and
looks like work."

Thomas Edison

List three opportunities that are currently presenting themselves to you:

1. _____

   _____

2. _____

   _____

3. _____

   _____

Write how you will capitalize on these opportunities.

Six Months Review:

_____

_____

_____

Quotation Source Information:

_____

_____

_____

February 17
August 18

"Choose a job that you like and you will
never have to work a day in your life."

Confucius

What is your dream job?

_____
_____
_____

What do you need to do to get that job?

_____
_____
_____

Six Months Review:

_____
_____
_____

Quotation Source Information:

_____
_____
_____

February 18
August 19

"History will be kind to me,
for I intend to write it."

Winston Churchill

List three ways in which you can write and publicize your life:

1. _____

   _____

2. _____

   _____

3. _____

   _____

Six Months Review:

_____

_____

_____

Quotation Source Information:

_____

_____

_____

February 19
August 20

> "When networking, stay-out of the *comfort-crowd* and don't gravitate into the *cozy-zone*. Meet new people."

Richard Possett

When you attend a networking gathering, what is your personal strategy for mingling and meeting new people?

_____
_____
_____

Six Months Review:

_____
_____
_____

Quotation Source Information:

_____
_____
_____

February 20
August 21

"The world hates change, yet it is the only thing that has brought progress."

Charles Kettering

List three perceived changes that you can be involved in:

1. _____
   _____

2. _____
   _____

3. _____
   _____

Get involved!!!

Six Months Review:

_____
_____
_____

Quotation Source Information:

_____
_____
_____

February 21
August 22

"I always do things I can't do,
that's how I get to do them."

Pablo Picasso

List three things that you have always wanted to do but couldn't:

1. _____
   _____

2. _____
   _____

3. _____
   _____

Do them!!!

Six Months Review:

_____
_____
_____

Quotation Source Information:

_____
_____
_____

February 22
August 23

"Minds are like parachutes, they only function when open."

Thomas Dewar

List three areas in which you are closed-minded:

1. _____
   _____

2. _____
   _____

3. _____
   _____

Open your mind today!!!

Six Months Review:

_____
_____
_____

Quotation Source Information:

_____
_____
_____

February 23
August 24

> "The sure way to do many things is to do
> only one thing at a time."

Mozart

What is one thing that you must get done today?

_____
_____
_____

Do it today!!!

Six Months Review:

_____
_____
_____

Quotation Source Information:

_____
_____
_____

February 24
August 25

"Only a mediocre person is at his best."

Somerset Maugham

List one area in your life that you can improve today:

_____

_____

Write an action plan and begin the improvement today!!!

Six Months Review:

_____

_____

_____

Quotation Source Information:

_____

_____

_____

February 25
August 26

> "If the only tool you have is a hammer, you
> tend to see every problem as a nail."

Abraham Maslow

List every *tool* you have available to conquer any problem that you may
encounter:

_____
_____
_____
_____

Six Months Review:

_____
_____
_____

Quotation Source Information:

_____
_____
_____

February 26
August 27

"Consider the postage stamp; it secures
success through its ability to stick to one
thing till it gets there."

Josh Billings

List three projects that you have started but never completed. Next to each project, write one thing that you will do today to complete the project and list a project completion date:

1. _____

_____

2. _____

_____

3. _____

_____

Six Months Review:

_____

_____

_____

Quotation Source Information:

_____

_____

_____

February 27
August 28

> "If you are going to be a successful duck hunter, you must go to where the ducks are."

Paul "Bear" Bryant

List three places where your target customers frequent:

1. _____
   _____

2. _____
   _____

3. _____
   _____

Six Months Review:

_____
_____
_____

Quotation Source Information:

_____
_____
_____

February 28
August 29

> "You live only once,
> but if you work it right,
> once is enough."

Joe Lewis

List three ways that you can enhance your life:

1. _____
_____

2. _____
_____

3. _____
_____

Six Months Review:

_____
_____
_____

Quotation Source Information:

_____
_____
_____

February 29
August 30

"If you can dream it, you can do it."

Walt Disney

List your three biggest dreams:

1. _____
_____

2. _____
_____

3. _____
_____

Six Months Review:

_____
_____
_____

Quotation Source Information:

_____
_____
_____

March 1
August 31

> "You can complain about your weight, or
> you can do something about it.
> Which do you choose?"

Unknown

How much do you want to weigh? _____

List three things you can do to achieve that weight:

1. _____
   _____

2. _____
   _____

3. _____
   _____

Six Months Review:

_____
_____
_____

March 2
September 1

> "My goal as a networker is to pass at least one lead everyday to one person in my network."

Peter Biadasz

Who did you pass a lead to yesterday?

_____

Who are you going to pass a lead to today?

_____

Six Months Review:

_____
_____
_____

Quotation Source Information:

_____
_____
_____

March 3
September 2

> "Good judgment comes from experience,
> and often experience comes from bad
> judgment."

Rita Mae Brown

List your three biggest blunders and what you learned from each:

1. _____

   _____

2. _____

   _____

3. _____

   _____

Six Months Review:

_____

_____

_____

Quotation Source Information:

_____

_____

_____

March 4
September 3

> "How wonderful it is that
> nobody need wait a single moment
> before starting to improve the world."
>
> **Anne Frank**

List three things you can do today to improve your world:

1. _____
   _____

2. _____
   _____

3. _____
   _____

Six Months Review:

_____
_____
_____

Quotation Source Information:

_____
_____
_____

March 5
September 4

> "If you don't make mistakes, you're not
> working on hard enough problems, and
> that's a big mistake."

F. Wikzek

List your three latest accomplishments and the mistakes that you made
while accomplishing them:

1. _____
   _____

2. _____
   _____

3. _____
   _____

Enjoy the accomplishments and learn from the mistakes!!!

Six Months Review:

_____
_____
_____

Quotation Source Information:

_____
_____
_____

March 6
September 5

"In the business world experience is paid in
two coins: cash and experience. Take the
experience first, the cash will come later."

Harold Geneen

List three ways that you can gain more experience in your profession:

1. _____
   _____

2. _____
   _____

3. _____
   _____

Six Months Review:

_____
_____
_____

Quotation Source Information:

_____
_____
_____

March 7
September 6

"The purpose of networking is to develop
symbiotic relationships producing
synergistic rewards."

Richard Possett

In your own words, restate the above definition of networking to help
you better understand what you are trying to accomplish in the
endeavor:

_____

_____

_____

Six Months Review:

_____

_____

_____

Quotation Source Information:

_____

_____

_____

March 8
September 7

> "You must have short-range goals
> that keep you from being frustrated
> by short-term failures."

Charles C. Noble

List three of your short-term goals:

1. _____

   _____

2. _____

   _____

3. _____

   _____

Now, write one thing that you will do before you go to bed tonight to help achieve each goal listed.

_____

_____

_____

_____

Six Months Review:

_____

_____

_____

Quotation Source Information:

_____

_____

_____

March 9
September 8

> "The number of people who are
> unemployed isn't as great as the number of
> people who aren't working."

Unknown

List five things you can do to ensure that you are working at your very best:

1. _____
   _____

2. _____
   _____

3. _____
   _____

4. _____
   _____

5. _____
   _____

Six Months Review:

_____
_____
_____

March 10
September 9

> "Some carve out a future, while others just whittle away their time."

Unknown

List your three most important long-term goals:

1. _____
   _____

2. _____
   _____

3. _____
   _____

Six Months Review:

_____
_____
_____

March 11
September 10

> "Talent is great but overrated.
> Determination, which stems from a belief
> in one's ability to succeed, is usually what
> separates the winners from the losers."

Unknown

On a scale of 1 to 10, with 10 being the best, rate yourself in your determination to be the best networker in your business community.

1   2   3   4   5   6   7   8   9   10

List three things that you can do to become a better networker:

1. _____

_____

2. _____

_____

3. _____

_____

Six Months Review:

_____

_____

_____

March 12
September 11

> "Mistakes are the usual bridge between inexperience and wisdom."
>
> **Phyllis Theroux**

List three areas in which you want more experience:

1. _____
   _____

2. _____
   _____

3. _____
   _____

Write your plan to gain the experience.

Six Months Review:

_____
_____
_____

Quotation Source Information:

_____
_____
_____

March 13
September 12

"The road to success is dotted with many tempting parking places."

Unknown

List two areas in which you are in a *parking place*. What are you going to do today to get out of those *parking places*?

1. _____

   _____

2. _____

   _____

Six Months Review:

_____

_____

_____

March 14
September 13

"Give me six hours to chop down a tree
and I will spend the first four
sharpening the axe."

Abraham Lincoln

How do you *sharpen your axe* daily?

_____
_____
_____
_____

Six Months Review:

_____
_____
_____

Quotation Source Information:

_____
_____
_____

March 15
September 14

"Conflict builds character, crisis defines it."

Steven V. Thulon

List five things that you like about your character:

1. _____
   _____

2. _____
   _____

3. _____
   _____

4. _____
   _____

5. _____
   _____

Six Months Review:

_____
_____
_____

Quotation Source Information:

_____
_____
_____

March 16
September 15

> "Now that it's all over, what did you really
> do yesterday that's worth mentioning."

Coleman Cox

List three memorable things you did yesterday:

1. _____
   _____

2. _____
   _____

3. _____
   _____

Make today memorable by doing memorable things.

Six Months Review:

_____
_____
_____

Quotation Source Information:

_____
_____
_____

March 17
September 16

> "You can tell more about a person by what they say about others than you can by what others say about them."

Leo Aikman

List five positive things that you consistently say about others:

1. _____
_____

2. _____
_____

3. _____
_____

4. _____
_____

5. _____
_____

Six Months Review:

_____
_____
_____

Quotation Source Information:

_____
_____
_____

March 18
September 17

> "All men who have achieved great things
> have been great dreamers."

Orison Swett Marden

List three of your greatest unfulfilled dreams:

1. _____
   _____

2. _____
   _____

3. _____
   _____

What will you do to fulfill each dream?

Six Months Review:

_____
_____
_____

Quotation Source Information:

_____
_____
_____

March 19
September 18

> "Business goes where it is wanted and stays
> where it is appreciated."

Unknown

List five ways that you show appreciation to your customers:

1. _____
   _____

2. _____
   _____

3. _____
   _____

4. _____
   _____

5. _____
   _____

Six Months Review:

_____
_____
_____

March 20
September 19

"Networkers build bridges, not walls."

Peter Biadasz

List one person that you have built a wall around and break that wall down today:

_____
_____
_____
_____

Six Months Review:

_____
_____
_____

Quotation Source Information:

_____
_____
_____

March 21
September 20

"Whatever you are, be a good one."

Abraham Lincoln

List three ways that you can be better at your profession:

1. _____
   _____

2. _____
   _____

3. _____
   _____

Six Months Review:

_____
_____
_____

Quotation Source Information:

_____
_____
_____

March 22
September 21

"If you want something done,
ask a busy person."

Unknown

List three people you know who have the strongest work ethic. Visit with each and learn how they achieve and maintain their intensity.

1. _____
   _____

2. _____
   _____

3. _____
   _____

Six Months Review:

_____
_____
_____

March 23
September 22

> "Kindness is the language which the deaf
> can hear and the blind can see."

Mark Twain

Perform five acts of kindness today. List them:

1. _____
_____

2. _____
_____

3. _____
_____

4. _____
_____

5. _____
_____

Six Months Review:

Quotation Source Information:

March 24
September 23

> "In networking, it's not who you know! In
> networking, it's who knows you!"

Richard Possett

Write down three new tactics and start dates of when you will use them
to become better known in the networking community.

1. _____
   _____

2. _____
   _____

3. _____
   _____

Six Months Review:

_____
_____
_____

Quotation Source Information:

_____
_____
_____

March 25
September 24

> "Feeling gratitude and not expressing it is like wrapping a present and not giving it."

William Ward

List five ways that you show gratitude to your family:

1. _____
   _____

2. _____
   _____

3. _____
   _____

4. _____
   _____

5. _____
   _____

Six Months Review:

_____
_____
_____

Quotation Source Information:

_____
_____
_____

March 26
September 25

> Bad habits are easier to abandon today
> than tomorrow.

Yiddish Proverb

List three of your *"baddest"* habits:

1. _____
   _____

2. _____
   _____

3. _____
   _____

Write a plan to eliminate each bad habit today!!!

Six Months Review:

_____
_____
_____

Quotation Source Information:

_____
_____
_____

March 27
September 26

"You control your life
by controlling your time."

Conrad Hilton

List five ways that you can improve your time management skills:

1. _____

_____

2. _____

_____

3. _____

_____

4. _____

_____

5. _____

_____

Six Months Review:

_____

_____

_____

Quotation Source Information:

_____

_____

_____

March 28
September 27

"Don't get bored with doing the basics."

Richard Possett

List five things you can do to increase your participation in networking meetings:

1. _____
   _____

2. _____
   _____

3. _____
   _____

4. _____
   _____

5. _____
   _____

Do them!!!

Six Months Review:

_____
_____
_____

Quotation Source Information:

_____
_____
_____

March 29
September 28

"If you want to be happy, be."

Leo Tolstoy

List five things that you are happy about in your life:

1. _____

_____

2. _____

_____

3. _____

_____

4. _____

_____

5. _____

_____

Six Months Review:

_____

_____

_____

Quotation Source Information:

_____

_____

_____

March 30
September 29

"Be the change that you want to see in the world."

Mahatma Gandhi

If you could change one thing in your world, what would it be?

_____

Write an action plan to initiate that change:

_____
_____
_____
_____

Six Months Review:

_____
_____
_____

Quotation Source Information:

_____
_____
_____

March 31
September 30

"Instead of counting your days,
make your days count."

Unknown

List three things that you can do today to make this day memorable:

1. _____
   _____

2. _____
   _____

3. _____
   _____

Six Months Review:

_____
_____
_____

April 1
October 1

"If you reveal your secrets to the wind, you should not blame the wind for revealing them to the trees."

Kahil Gibran

List three of your most trusted relationships:

1. _____
   _____

2. _____
   _____

3. _____
   _____

Can others trust you to keep secrets?

Six Months Review:

_____
_____
_____

Quotation Source Information:

_____
_____
_____

April 2
October 2

"Nine tenths of education is encouragement."

Anatole France

List five encouraging things that your teachers did when you were in school:

1. _____
   _____

2. _____
   _____

3. _____
   _____

4. _____
   _____

5. _____
   _____

Now, list next to each item the name of a person that you will encourage in the same manner.

Six Months Review:

_____
_____
_____

Quotation Source Information:

_____
_____
_____

April 3
October 3

> "If your actions inspire others to dream
> more, learn more, do more and become
> more, you are a leader."

John Quincy Adams

List one unfulfilled dream and one thing you can do today to help that dream become a reality:

_____

_____

List one topic that you would like to learn more about and a book, website, etc. that you can look at today to learn something about that topic:

_____

_____

Six Months Review:

_____

_____

_____

Quotation Source Information:

_____

_____

_____

April 4
October 4

> "A man can succeed at almost anything for which
> he has unlimited enthusiasm."
>
> Unknown

List three things about which you have the most enthusiasm:

1. _____
   _____

2. _____
   _____

3. _____
   _____

Six Months Review:

_____
_____
_____

April 5
October 5

"Who received a lead from me today?"

Peter Biadasz

List three people that you are going to pass a lead to today:

1. _____
   _____

2. _____
   _____

3. _____
   _____

Six Months Review:

_____
_____
_____

Quotation Source Information:

_____
_____
_____

April 6
October 6

"Small minds discuss people, average minds discuss events, great minds discuss ideas."

Anonymous

List three original ideas that you have and develop them usefully:

1. _____

_____

2. _____

_____

3. _____

_____

Six Months Review:

_____

_____

_____

April 7
October 7

"We take the hamburger business more seriously than anyone else."

Ray Kroc

How do you take your business more seriously than anyone else?

_____
_____
_____
_____

Six Months Review:

_____
_____
_____

Quotation Source Information:

_____
_____
_____

April 8
October 8

"When prosperity comes, do not use it all."

Confucius

How much money do you save daily, weekly, monthly, yearly?

_____

_____

How much money do you _want to_ save daily, weekly, monthly, yearly?

_____

_____

_____

Six Months Review:

_____

_____

_____

Quotation Source Information:

_____

_____

_____

April 9
October 9

> "For most men, life is a search for the
> proper manila envelope in which to get
> themselves filed."

Clifton Fadiman

List three of the niches you feel you have in life:

1. _____
   _____

2. _____
   _____

3. _____
   _____

Six Months Review:

_____
_____
_____

Quotation Source Information:

_____
_____
_____

April 10
October 10

"A man is not old as long as
he is seeking something."

Jean Rostand

What are three things that you want to do or achieve in your lifetime?

1. _____

_____

2. _____

_____

3. _____

_____

Write one thing that you will do today to move one step closer to accomplishing each item listed:

_____

_____

Six Months Review:

_____

_____

_____

Quotation Source Information:

_____

_____

_____

April 11
October 11

"It is not enough to do your best: you must know what to do, and then do your best."

W. Edwards Deming

List three things you do to always achieve your best.

1. _____
   _____

2. _____
   _____

3. _____
   _____

Do you do these things at the right time every time?

Six Months Review:

_____
_____
_____

Quotation Source Information:

_____
_____
_____

April 12
October 12

"Dream as if you'll live forever, live as if you'll die tomorrow."

James Dean

What is your biggest unfulfilled dream?

_____

_____

How can it be fulfilled?

_____

_____

Six Months Review:

_____

_____

_____

Quotation Source Information:

_____

_____

_____

April 13
October 13

"Networking is about *you and me*. It's the
state of *we* vis-à-vis the status of me. Thus,
we plug others to pitch ourselves."

Richard Possett

Can you name three fellow networkers whom you have actively pro-
moted? If not, target three and aggressively promote them.

1. _____

   _____

2. _____

   _____

3. _____

   _____

Six Months Review:

_____

_____

_____

Quotation Source Information:

_____

_____

_____

April 14
October 14

"To keep a lamp burning, you have to keep putting oil in it."

Mother Teresa

List three types of *oil* that you put into your *lamp*?

1. _____

_____

2. _____

_____

3. _____

_____

Six Months Review:

_____

_____

_____

Quotation Source Information:

_____

_____

_____

April 15
October 15

"Knowledge is the process of piling up facts; wisdom lies in their simplification."

Martin Fischer

List three important facts and the best way to teach those facts to another in your network:

1. _____
   _____

2. _____
   _____

3. _____
   _____

Six Months Review:

_____
_____
_____

Quotation Source Information:

_____
_____
_____

April 16
October 16

Be not afraid of growing slowly,
be afraid of standing still.

Chinese Proverb

List three areas of your life in which you are *standing still*:

1. _____
   _____

2. _____
   _____

3. _____
   _____

List one way that you can gain momentum to grow in each of these areas.

Six Months Review:

_____
_____
_____

Quotation Source Information:

_____
_____
_____

April 17
October 17

> "Be curious always! For knowledge will not
> acquire you: you must acquire it."
>
> **Sudie Back**

List three things that you have always been curious about:

1. _____

    _____

2. _____

    _____

3. _____

    _____

Next to each one, write how you will satisfy your curiosity.

Six Months Review:

_____

_____

_____

Quotation Source Information:

_____

_____

_____

April 18
October 18

"We could learn a lot from crayons: some
are sharp, some are pretty, some are dull,
some have weird names, and all are
different colors but they all have to learn to
live in the same box."

Unknown

List three things that you have learned in dealing with the diversity of
those in your daily life:

1. _____
   _____

2. _____
   _____

3. _____
   _____

Six Months Review:

_____
_____
_____

April 19
October 19

> ## "The art of teaching is the art of assisting discovery."

Mark Van Doren

List three areas in which you have expertise:

1. _____
   _____

2. _____
   _____

3. _____
   _____

Next to each area listed, write the name of someone whom you can share your information with.

Six Months Review:

_____
_____
_____

Quotation Source Information:

_____
_____
_____

April 20
October 20

"The more organized your network, the greater your effectiveness as a networker."

Peter Biadasz

Write one way that you can better organize your network:

_____

Six Months Review:

_____
_____
_____

Quotation Source Information:

_____
_____
_____

April 21
October 21

> "I do not think much of a man who is not
> wiser today than he was yesterday."

Abraham Lincoln

List three things that you learned yesterday:

1. _____
   _____

2. _____
   _____

3. _____
   _____

Six Months Review:

_____
_____
_____

Quotation Source Information:

_____
_____
_____

April 22
October 22

"Our networking vision is to create an everlasting circle of influence composed of a massive group of stakeholders dedicated to mutual growth and prosperity."

Richard Possett

List three ways in which you will become better known in your community:

1. _____

_____

2. _____

_____

3. _____

_____

Write a start date and action plan for each item listed.

Six Months Review:

_____

_____

_____

Quotation Source Information:

_____

_____

_____

April 23
October 23

"My success just evolved from working hard at the business at hand."

Johnny Carson

What is your main business?

_____

How can you improve your productivity by *five percent*?

_____
_____
_____
_____

Six Months Review:

_____
_____
_____

Quotation Source Information:

_____
_____
_____

April 24
October 24

"Fears are educated into us and can, if we
choose to, be educated out."

Karl Menninger

List your three greatest fears:

1. _____
   _____

2. _____
   _____

3. _____
   _____

Next to each fear write how you are going to overcome that fear. Enlist
the assistance of others if necessary.

Six Months Review:
_____
_____
_____

Quotation Source Information:
_____
_____
_____

April 25
October 25

> "In the case of good books, the point is not how many of them you can get through, but rather how many can get through to you."

Mortimer Adler

What is the best book you have ever read?

_____

What book do you want to read? Buy that book today!!!

_____

Six Months Review:

_____

_____

_____

Quotation Source Information:

_____

_____

_____

April 26
October 26

"The quality of a person's life is in direct proportion to their commitment to excellence, regardless of their chosen field."

Vince Lombardi

List three things that you do to ensure excellence in everything that you undertake:

1. _____

   _____

2. _____

   _____

3. _____

   _____

Six Months Review:

_____

_____

_____

Quotation Source Information:

_____

_____

_____

April 27
October 27

> "In the long run men hit
> only what they aim at."

Henry David Thoreau

List your one day, one week, one month and one year goals:

One day: _____

One week: _____

One month: _____

One year: _____

Six Months Review:
_____
_____
_____

Quotation Source Information:
_____
_____
_____

April 28
October 28

> "Blessed is the man who is too busy to worry in the daytime and too sleepy to worry at night."

Unknown

List three things that you can do to improve your time management skills:

1. _____
   _____

2. _____
   _____

3. _____
   _____

What time do you really want to go to bed at night? _____

Do it tonight!!

Six Months Review:

_____
_____
_____

April 29
October 29

> "The second half of a man's life is made up of nothing but the habits he has acquired during the first half."

Fyodor Dostoevsky

List three of your best habits:

1. _____
_____

2. _____
_____

3. _____
_____

List three of your worst habits:

1. _____
_____

2. _____
_____

3. _____
_____

Strengthen the first three habits and eliminate the last three habits today!!!

Six Months Review:

_____
_____
_____

Quotation Source Information:

_____
_____
_____

April 30
October 30

"Act as if what you do makes a difference. It does!"

William James

List three ways that you can be more enthusiastic about your family and work:

Family:
  1. _____
  2. _____
  3. _____

Work:
  1. _____
  2. _____
  3. _____

Six Months Review:
Family: _____

Work: _____

Quotation Source Information:
_____
_____
_____

May 1
October 31

"The secret of getting ahead is getting started."

Unknown

List three things that you have been procrastinating:

1. _____
   _____

2. _____
   _____

3. _____
   _____

Write down something that you will do *today* to accomplish each item.

Six Months Review:

_____
_____
_____

May 2
November 1

> "Take the time to come home
> to yourself everyday."

Robin Casarjean

List three things that you do for yourself daily:

1. _____
   _____
2. _____
   _____
3. _____
   _____

Six Months Review:

_____
_____
_____

Quotation Source Information:

_____
_____
_____

May 3
November 2

"Everything is an opportunity for someone in your networking group."

Peter Biadasz

Today, be aware of how people in your network can improve the lives of everyone that you come in contact with. Write down three people that can benefit from people in your network:

1. _____
   _____

2. _____
   _____

3. _____
   _____

Six Months Review:

_____
_____
_____

Quotation Source Information:

_____
_____
_____

May 4
November 3

When you throw dirt, you lose ground.

Texan Proverb

List the last three criticisms that you extended and reword them to be helpful and constructive information:

1. _____
   _____

2. _____
   _____

3. _____
   _____

Six Months Review:

_____
_____
_____

Quotation Source Information:

_____
_____
_____

May 5
November 4

"Stand-out from the crowd by personally
differentiating yourself; and, create a special
marketing offer for your company. This is
how you brand you and what you do!"

Richard Possett

Describe your personal brand and your company's special marketing
offer that makes you unique with remarkable trade appeal:

_____
_____
_____

Six Months Review:

_____
_____
_____

Quotation Source Information:

_____
_____
_____

May 6
November 5

"The best way to become acquainted with a subject is to write a book about it."

Benjamin Disraeli

List three things that you passionately know a lot about:

1. _____
   _____
2. _____
   _____
3. _____
   _____

Write an article on each item. If you have a lot of information write a series of articles that may be used as the foundation in writing a book.

Six Months Review:

_____
_____

Quotation Source Information:

_____
_____
_____

May 7
November 6

"Some look at tomorrow as another day...
I look at it as a second chance."

Unknown

List three things that you did not do yesterday. Do them today now that you have a second chance.

1. _____
   _____

2. _____
   _____

3. _____
   _____

Six Months Review:

_____
_____
_____

May 8
November 7

"Do not hire a man who
does your work for money,
but him who does it for the love of it."

Henry David Thoreau

List three people that have a passion for what they do:

1. _____
   _____

2. _____
   _____

3. _____
   _____

Find out how they fuel their passion.

Six Months Review:

_____
_____
_____

Quotation Source Information:

_____
_____
_____

May 9
November 8

"Time is the most valuable thing
a man can spend."

Theophrastus

List three ways that you can improve your time management skills:

1. _____

_____

2. _____

_____

3. _____

_____

Six Months Review:

_____

_____

_____

Quotation Source Information:

_____

_____

_____

If you want to be respected, you must respect yourself.

Spanish Proverb

List three things that you respect about yourself:

1. _____
   _____

2. _____
   _____

3. _____
   _____

Six Months Review:

_____
_____
_____

Quotation Source Information:

_____
_____
_____

May 11
November 10

> "Never discourage anyone...who
> continually makes progress,
> no matter how slow."

Plato

List three of the hardest workers that you know:

1. _____
   _____

2. _____
   _____

3. _____
   _____

Let them know that you appreciate their work ethic.

Six Months Review:

_____
_____
_____

Quotation Source Information:

_____
_____
_____

"Bite off more than you can chew, then
chew it. Plan more than you can do,
then do it."

Unknown

List three of your primary goals:

1. _____
   _____

2. _____
   _____

3. _____
   _____

Increase each goal by *five percent*.

Six Months Review:

_____
_____
_____

May 13
November 12

"In networking, step forward; take charge;
lead by example; follow-through;
give it your all; start to finish; and,
most essentially, give to get."

Richard Possett

List three things that you can do to be a more productive networker:

1. _____

   _____

2. _____

   _____

3. _____

   _____

Six Months Review:

_____

_____

_____

Quotation Source Information:

_____

_____

_____

May 14
November 13

"By perseverance the snail reached the ark."

Charles Spurgeon

List three people you know that have a "don't quit" temperament:

1. _____

2. _____

3. _____

Find out what keeps them going no matter what the circumstance.

Six Months Review:

_____
_____
_____

Quotation Source Information:

_____
_____
_____

May 15
November 14

> "When people talk, listen completely.
> Most people never listen."

Ernest Hemingway

Rate your listening skills on a scale of 1 to 10.

| 1 | 2 | 3 | 4 | 5 | 6 | 7 | 8 | 9 | 10 |

List three ways that you can improve your listening skills.

1. _____
   _____
2. _____
   _____
3. _____
   _____

Six Months Review:

_____
_____
_____

Quotation Source Information:

_____
_____
_____

May 16
November 15

> "The happiness of a man in this life does
> not consist in the absence but in the
> mastery of his passions."

Alfred Lord Tennyson

List your three greatest passions along with what you need to do to take
them to the next level of mastery:

1. _____

   _____

2. _____

   _____

3. _____

   _____

Six Months Review:

_____

_____

_____

Quotation Source Information:

_____

_____

_____

May 17
November 16

"Knowledge is power."

Francis Bacon

List your three greatest areas of expertise:

1. _____

   _____

2. _____

   _____

3. _____

   _____

Six Months Review:

_____

_____

_____

Quotation Source Information:

_____

_____

_____

May 18
November 17

> "Footprints on the sands of time
> are not made by sitting down."
>
> **Unknown**

List three things that you do to ensure that you are a person of action:

1. _____
   _____

2. _____
   _____

3. _____
   _____

Six Months Review:

_____
_____
_____

May 19
November 18

"They can conquer who believe they can."

Virgil

List your biggest fear:

_____
_____
_____
_____

Create an action plan to overcome that fear.

Six Months Review:

_____
_____
_____

Quotation Source Information:

_____
_____
_____

May 20
November 19

> "You do not have to have
> the title of manager to be the
> mood manager of your office."

Peter Biadasz

List one way that you can be a positive (attitude) influence in your office
and at home:

Home:

_____

_____

Office:

_____

_____

Six Months Review:

_____

_____

_____

Quotation Source Information:

_____

_____

_____

May 21
November 20

> "A sobering thought: what if, at this very
> moment, I am living up to my full
> potential?"

Jane Wagner

List three areas of your life in which you are living up to your potential
and three areas that you are not living up to your potential:

1. _____
   _____
2. _____
   _____
3. _____
   _____

1. _____
   _____
2. _____
   _____
3. _____
   _____

Six Months Review:

_____
_____
_____

Quotation Source Information:

_____
_____
_____

May 22
November 21

> "To the world you might be one person, but
> to one person you might be the world."

Unknown

List five people who think you are important to them. Let them know today how important they are to you.

1. _____
   _____

2. _____
   _____

3. _____
   _____

4. _____
   _____

5. _____
   _____

Six Months Review:

_____
_____
_____

May 23
November 22

> "We make a living by what we get. We make
> a life by what we give."

Winston Churchill

List five ways that you can give today.

1. _____

   _____

2. _____

   _____

3. _____

   _____

4. _____

   _____

5. _____

   _____

Six Months Review:

_____

_____

_____

Quotation Source Information:

_____

_____

_____

May 24
November 23

"The measure of success is not whether you
have a tough problem to deal with, but
whether it is the same problem
you had last year."

John Foster Dulles

List five of your current problems:

1. _____
_____
2. _____
_____
3. _____
_____
4. _____
_____
5. _____
_____

Did you have any of these same problems 12 months ago? If so, eliminate that problem immediately.

Six Months Review:

_____
_____
_____

Quotation Source Information:

_____
_____
_____

May 25
November 24

"Everyone has a photographic memory,
some just have film."

Unknown

List three ways that you can improve your short-term and long-term memory:

1. _____

   _____

2. _____

   _____

3. _____

   _____

Six Months Review:

_____

_____

_____

May 26
November 25

"They may forget what you said, but they
will never forget how you made them feel."

Carl Buechner

List three people that make you feel good about yourself:

1. _____

2. _____

3. _____

Make three people feel good about themselves today!!!

Six Months Review:

_____
_____
_____

Quotation Source Information:

_____
_____
_____

May 27
November 26

"Never let the fear of striking out get in your way."

Babe Ruth

List your three biggest fears in becoming successful:

1. _____

   _____

2. _____

   _____

3. _____

   _____

Overcome those fears today!!!

Six Months Review:

_____

_____

_____

Quotation Source Information:

_____

_____

_____

May 28
November 27

"A man who dares waste one hour of his life
has not discovered the value of life."

Charles Darwin

List your five biggest time wasters:

1. _____

2. _____

3. _____

4. _____

5. _____

Eliminate those time wasters today!!!

Six Months Review:

_____
_____
_____

Quotation Source Information:

_____
_____
_____

May 29
November 28

"Make a decision, then do it, no matter how
small—toward accomplishing
what you want."

Unknown

List the biggest thing that you want to accomplish:

_____

_____

List one thing that you will do today to accomplish that task:

_____

Six Months Review:

_____

_____

_____

May 30
November 29

"Meeting people formally is like viewing a
house without going inside."

Charlie Chaplin

List three ways that you can deepen your existing relationships:

1. _____

_____

2. _____

_____

3. _____

_____

Six Months Review:

_____

_____

_____

Quotation Source Information:

_____

_____

_____

May 31
November 30

"I have never let my schooling interfere with my education."

Mark Twain

List five ways that you can further educate yourself today:

1. _____
   _____
2. _____
   _____
3. _____
   _____
4. _____
   _____
5. _____
   _____

Six Months Review:

_____
_____
_____

Quotation Source Information:

_____
_____
_____

June 1
December 1

"Time flies.
It's up to you to be the navigator."

Robert Orben

List three ways that you can manage your time better:

1. _____

2. _____

3. _____

Six Months Review:

_____
_____
_____

Quotation Source Information:

_____
_____
_____

June 2
December 2

Fall seven times, stand up eight.

Japanese Proverb

List three reasons to always get up that eighth time:

1. _____
_____

2. _____
_____

3. _____
_____

Six Months Review:

_____
_____
_____

Quotation Source Information:

_____
_____
_____

June 3
December 3

"Enthusiasm spells the difference between
mediocrity and accomplishment."

Norman Vincent Peale

Who is the most enthusiastic person that you know?

_____

Meet with them to find out how they stay so enthusiastic. Write down
their *secrets* for enthusiasm.

_____
_____
_____

Six Months Review:

_____
_____
_____

Quotation Source Information:

_____
_____
_____

June 4
December 4

"Networking is something that you do.
Being a networker is someone that you are."

Peter Biadasz

List two things that you are going to do today to become a better net-worker than you were yesterday:

1. _____
   _____

2. _____
   _____

Six Months Review:

_____
_____
_____

Quotation Source Information:

_____
_____
_____

June 5
December 5

"If you can't see the bright side of life, polish the dull side."

Unknown

List three boring parts of your life:

1. _____

2. _____

3. _____

What can you do to add excitement to each of these areas?

Six Months Review:

_____
_____
_____

June 6
December 6

"The trouble with being punctual is that nobody's there to appreciate it."

Franklin Jones

List three ways that you can improve your punctuality habits:

1. _____
   _____

2. _____
   _____

3. _____
   _____

Six Months Review:

_____
_____
_____

Quotation Source Information:

_____
_____
_____

June 7
December 7

"I love deadlines. I especially like the
whooshing sound they make as they go
flying by."

Unknown

List your three most dreaded deadlines:

1. _____
   _____

2. _____
   _____

3. _____
   _____

Write how you are going to meet those deadlines.

Six Months Review:

_____
_____
_____

June 8
December 8

"In the end it is not the years in your life
that count, it's the life in your years."

Abraham Lincoln

List three regrets that you have in your life so far. Next to each regret,
write what you will do today to start correcting each regret.

1. _____

2. _____

3. _____

Six Months Review:

_____

Quotation Source Information:

_____

June 9
December 9

"I don't suffer from stress, I'm a carrier."

Unknown

List three ways that you relieve/eliminate stress:

1. _____
   _____

2. _____
   _____

3. _____
   _____

Six Months Review:

_____
_____
_____

June 10
December 10

> "The artist is nothing without the gift, but the gift is nothing without work."
>
> **Emile Zola**

List three of your greatest gifts (talents):

1. _____
   _____

2. _____
   _____

3. _____
   _____

How will you further develop each gift?

Six Months Review:

_____
_____
_____

Quotation Source Information:

_____
_____
_____

June 11
December 11

"When you do the common things in life in
an uncommon way, you will command the
attention of the world."

George Washington Carver

List three everyday things that you love to do:

1. _____
   _____

2. _____
   _____

3. _____
   _____

How can you do each thing better?

Six Months Review:

_____
_____
_____

Quotation Source Information:

_____
_____
_____

June 12
December 12

"It's kind of fun to do the impossible."

Walt Disney

List three things that you think would be impossible for you to accomplish:

1. _____
   _____

2. _____
   _____

3. _____
   _____

Devise a plan to accomplish each item listed.

Six Months Review:

_____
_____
_____

Quotation Source Information:

_____
_____
_____

June 13
December 13

"Experience is simply the name we give to our mistakes."

Oscar Wilde

List three mistakes from which you learned something:

1. _____
   _____

2. _____
   _____

3. _____
   _____

Share those experiences with someone today.

Six Months Review:

_____
_____
_____

Quotation Source Information:

_____
_____
_____

June 14
December 14

"If you have knowledge,
let others light their candles at it."

Margaret Fuller

List three things that you have much knowledge about:

1. _____

   _____

2. _____

   _____

3. _____

   _____

Share this knowledge with someone verbally or in writing.

Six Months Review:

_____

_____

_____

Quotation Source Information:

_____

_____

_____

June 15
December 15

"Good thoughts are no better than good dreams, unless they be executed."

Ralph Waldo Emerson

List three of the biggest dreams for your life and set a timeline to realize each dream.

1. _____
   _____
2. _____
   _____
3. _____
   _____

Six Months Review:

_____
_____
_____

Quotation Source Information:

_____
_____
_____

June 16
December 16

"You can't wait for inspiration; you have to go after it with a club."

Jack London

What is one thing that you wish you were passionate about?

_____

Make a strong effort to develop a passion for that.

Six Months Review:

_____
_____
_____

Quotation Source Information:

_____
_____
_____

June 17
December 17

"The reason some people don't go very far
in life is because they sidestep opportunity
and shake hands with procrastination."

Unknown

List two things you have been procrastinating and list one action that you will do today to complete each thing.

1. _____
   _____
2. _____
   _____

Six Months Review:

_____
_____
_____

June 18
December 18

> "Treat people as if they were what they
> ought to be and you help them to become
> what they are capable of being."

Goethe

List five people you know who have much unused potential. How can you treat each of these individuals to help them achieve their true potential?

1. _____
   _____

2. _____
   _____

3. _____
   _____

4. _____
   _____

5. _____
   _____

Six Months Review:

_____
_____
_____

Quotation Source Information:

_____
_____
_____

June 19
December 19

"A minute's success pays a failure of years."

Robert Browning

List your three greatest successes:

1. _____

   _____

2. _____

   _____

3. _____

   _____

Six Months Review:

_____

_____

_____

Quotation Source Information:

_____

_____

_____

June 20
December 20

"Self-confidence is the first requisite to great undertakings."

Samuel Johnson

List three things that you do to feel better about yourself:

1. _____
_____

2. _____
_____

3. _____
_____

Six Months Review:
_____
_____
_____

Quotation Source Information:
_____
_____
_____

June 21
December 21

> When that character of a man is not clear to
> you look at his friends.

Japanese Proverb

List your three closest friends:

1. _____
   _____

2. _____
   _____

3. _____
   _____

How do you feel about the character of each friend?

Six Months Review:

_____
_____
_____

Quotation Source Information:

_____
_____
_____

June 22
December 22

"Change your thoughts and
you can change the world."

Norman Vincent Peale

List three positive things that you think about daily:

1. _____

   _____

2. _____

   _____

3. _____

   _____

Six Months Review:

_____

_____

_____

Quotation Source Information:

_____

_____

_____

June 23
December 23

"If a mistake is not a stepping stone,
it is just a mistake."

Eli Siegel

List three things that you have learned from recent mistakes:

1. _____

2. _____

3. _____

Six Months Review:

_____
_____
_____

Quotation Source Information:

_____
_____
_____

June 24
December 24

"Both optimists and pessimists contribute
to our society, the optimist invents the
airplane and the pessimist the parachute."

Gil Stern

List three optimists and three pessimists in your life:

Optimists:
1. _____
   _____
2. _____
   _____
3. _____
   _____

Pessimists:
1. _____
   _____
2. _____
   _____
3. _____
   _____

What do you learn from each person? Are you an optimist or a pessimist?

Six Months Review:

_____
_____
_____

Quotation Source Information:

_____
_____
_____

June 25
December 25

"I plan on living forever. So far, so good."

Unknown

List three things that you do to ensure that you have a high quality of life:

1. _____

2. _____

3. _____

Six Months Review:

_____
_____
_____

June 26
December 26

"Don't get your knickers in a knot. Nothing is solved and it just makes you walk funny."

Kathryn Carpenter

List three ways that you overcome frustration:

1. _____
   _____

2. _____
   _____

3. _____
   _____

Six Months Review:

_____
_____
_____

Quotation Source Information:

_____
_____
_____

June 27
December 27

"Am I not destroying my enemies when I make friends of them?"

Abraham Lincoln

List your three biggest "enemies."

1. _____

_____

2. _____

_____

3. _____

_____

Write how you are going to turn them into friends. Do it!!!

Six Months Review:

_____

_____

_____

Quotation Source Information:

_____

_____

_____

June 28
December 28

> "Opportunity often knocks on the door, but it has never been known to turn the knob and walk right into your living room and sit down with you."

Richard Possett

List three opportunities that are facing you right now:

1. _____

   _____

2. _____

   _____

3. _____

   _____

Which one must you take advantage of?

Six Months Review:

_____

_____

_____

Quotation Source Information:

_____

_____

_____

June 29
December 29

> "By being a networker you are a total
> resource for everyone that you come in
> contact with."

Peter Biadasz

Go through the telephone book yellow pages and write down three
industries that you do not have in your network. Contact people in
those industries to add to your network.

1. _____
   _____

2. _____
   _____

3. _____
   _____

Six Months Review:

_____
_____
_____

Quotation Source Information:

_____
_____
_____

June 30
December 30

"Keep in mind always the present
you are constructing. It should be
the future you want."

Alice Walker

Where do you want your life to be in one week, one month, six months,
one year and five years?

One Week: _____

One Month: _____

Six Months: _____

One Year: _____

Five Years: _____

Six Months Review:

_____

_____

_____

Quotation Source Information:

_____

_____

_____

July 1
December 31

"God grant me the serenity to accept the
people I cannot change, the courage to
change the one I can, and the wisdom to
know it's me."

Unknown

(A variation of an excerpt from "The Serenity Prayer" by Reinhold Neibuhr)

List one thing that you want to change about you.

_____

_____

Do it!!!!!!

Six Months Review:

_____

_____

_____

Quotation Source Information:

_____

_____

_____

Congratulations!!!

You have completed a milestone and made a major investment in yourself. If you are in the first six months of this book, you have learned much about yourself and the qualities that are needed to be a powerful networker. If you just completed the last six months of this book, you have completed a year long journey that has polished the skills and established habits needed to further your journey down the road of powerful networking.

Now that you have completed this journey, share it with others in your network. By helping your network to become more powerful, you make yourself a more powerful networker.

Networkers are givers! By completing this volume, know that you have much to give to everyone that you come in contact with in your daily life.

Again, congratulations!!!!!

Peter Biadasz and Richard Possett

Conclusion

You have just finished the footwork, so now is the time to put it to real work. That is, make it work for you in networking. You have absorbed the quotations and learned about the author or the quote source. In the first six months, you have fully completed each daily lesson. In the second six months, you have carefully reviewed the assignments and made the appropriate adjustments. During this period of time, you have practiced what you have learned. All these concluded tasks have made you a more powerful person. You did it on your own. You did it in private. Now, fully infuse that power into your daily public life. Release the power of networking into your personal and professional living life activities.

You already know that powerful people are powerful networkers. You read about them in books, magazines and newspapers. Everyday, you see them on television and hear them on radio. So, if you have carefully read this book and diligently completed the exercises, then you have made the choice to be powerful. And, success and power are nurtured by the same essential quality, powerful networking. Now, go forth and network knowing you have the power of success, for powerful people are powerful networkers.

About the Authors

Peter Biadasz (pronounced *bee-ahd-ish*) has been participating, tutoring and mentoring with networking groups since 1989. During this time, he has functioned as president, consultant, speaker, and as a very active member in these groups. Peter has been a networker all of his life and is considered a master networker by his peers. Occasionally, Peter has been known to utilize his professional trumpet talent to liven up speaking engagements.

Peter is a graduate of Florida State University. His passion for and expertise in the areas of networking groups and people has aided many fellow networkers in getting more leads from networking. Experience has shown that the groups working with Peter have an increase in the quality and quantity of leads passed. Furthermore, an excitement for networking, never before seen, emerges from the groups as members transform into distinguished and mature networkers.

The father of an incredible son and precious daughter, Peter is also the author of MORE LEADS: The Complete Handbook for TIPS Groups, Leads Groups, and Networking Groups. Please visit with Peter at www.getmoreleads.net.

Richard Possett is an experienced entrepreneur and seasoned sales and marketing executive from the financial and insurance services industries. As a successful businessman, Richard has spent decades in the field of marketing, effectively using the art of networking in the sales process. Currently, he is a Principal and the Executive Marketing Director of Navigator Home Loan, a comprehensive provider of residential home loans to consumers and commercial loans to businesses.

Born and raised in Grand Rapids, Michigan, Richard lived and worked for five years in Los Angeles, California before moving to the Midwest where he and his family have resided for the last eighteen years. He served in the United States Army during the Vietnam War. Richard has been married to his wife, Marilyn, for more than 41 years. He has three adult children (Nicole, Richard and Michael); son-in-law Daryl; and, two grandchildren (Braden and Rebekah). His hobbies are writing, reading and walking with his wife and their two golden retrievers.

As a graduate from Western Michigan University, Richard received a BBA Degree earning a major in accountancy. He is a CPA, accredited mortgage loan originator, financialist and past SEC-registered securities representative and licensed insurance agent. Richard is the author of *Gargantuan Networking; Hey! What's Your Score?; Clan Vanposetski; Possetts Powerful Pithy Pointers; The Family History of Margaret Mary Frauenfelder-Van Dyke; Living Life; Introspectively Speaking;* and, *Introspectively Inspired.* Please visit with Richard at rpossett@sbcglobal.net.

Index of Individuals Quoted

Index of Topics Quoted

Note: Many quotes may fit into more than one category.

978-0-595-37723-7
0-595-37723-8